A special thanks
to everyone
who has helped make
Know Yourself
what it is today.

Dear Reader

Knowing yourself is truly the beginning of all wisdom. We give young learners the building blocks they need to start their unique journey of self-discovery: an understanding of human anatomy — literally how we are put together. Knowledge of one's own human body is an empowering context on which anyone can build.

Learning about the body and mind at a young age sets the foundation for honoring one's physical form, develops self-esteem and self-confidence, and begins the discovery of who we are meant to be in this world.

Now that's real power.

The Know Yourself Team

Quick-Start Guide
Hello Know Yourselfers!

Follow these steps to start a new journey and explore the lymphatic system. Have fun on this quest and remember - Keep your wits about you!

1

Grab your atlatl.
We're going to Tenochtitlan.

Find Mexico City on your atlas, or find an online map of the world.

2

Read Time Skaters Adventure 10

Pinky, Naz, and Sketch are back in the past! With the help of Montezuma the Younger, can they find the next piece of the puzzle in time?

3

Get equipped!

Search for your supplies listed on the home inventory page.

Table of Contents

Hello Adventurer!

Welcome to Adventure 10 - The Lymphatic System.

In this workbook, you will learn about Tenochtitlan, Mexico and your body's Lymphatic System. There will be information to read, activities to complete, and quizzes to take when you are ready to challenge yourself! Take your time along the way - spend as much or as little time as you like on each activity.

Good luck, and have fun!

Destination:
Ancient Mexico

THE TIME TRAVEL CLOCK READS

1476

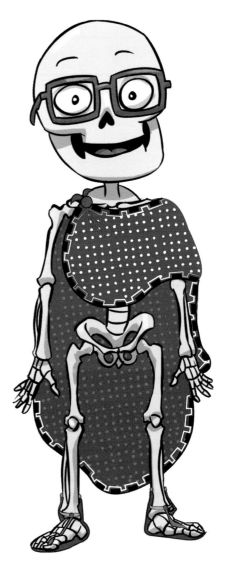

**Get ready
to start flowing!**

The Lymphatic System

Maintaining blood pressure and seeking intruders, this system is a part of the body's immune system.

Ancient Mexico in 1476

The vast metropolis of Tenochtitlan started as a tiny island, but grew to an impressive size.

Montezuma II

He ruled over a nation of great engineering projects, advanced knowledge and vast territory.

UNITED STATES

MEXICO

Gulf of Mexico

MEXICO CITY

Pacific Ocean

Guatemala

Ximpopanoltih*

(That means "Welcome!" in Nahuatl)
The language of the Ancient Aztecs.
Say it like this: "shee-mo-puh-NOT-tee"
The strongest syllable is shown in **CAPITALS** and **red.**

Enter this portal for....

Time Skaters Adventure 10
Lymphin' Large

LYMPHIN' LARGE

I can't believe you were just in the future! In space!

I know! It was just like an episode of...

Cosmic Voyager!

BUMP!

Cosmic what?

I can't believe you've never seen *Cosmic Voyager!*

It's all about these really smart people exploring space and making the galaxy a better place.

I don't think Pinky would agree with the show's Core Protocol.

"Never interfere with another culture's timeline!"

Even if people are in danger.

You're right, I don't agree with that.

FLASH!

Speaking of interference, I detect some in the space-time continuum.

HANK!!!

Bounski sees a problem with that plan.

The Portal won't close!

It must be supercharged from having five Time Skaters in one place!

But we have to go. We don't know when we'll get another lead like this.

Bounski and I can guard the Portal until it closes.

The girls can go with you, Hank.

That is a smart idea. Thank you, Stokely.

Alright, here goes.

I hope we get to go to space again!

Well, this is some of the freshest water we've landed in.

Maybe we are in the futu--

Mutants! We are back in space!

No, they've got human minds. They're ordinary people.

Just with very pointy weapons.

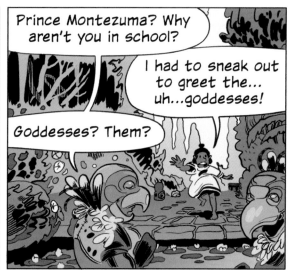

That was close! Good thing you guys showed up like you were destined to!

Destined to?

When I saw that calendar painted on your...whatever that is, I knew we were destined to meet!

But **you** don't really think we're **goddesses.**

You just said that so you wouldn't get in **trouble.**

Well those guys take the law so **seriously.**

"Every boy in the city has to go to school." Booooooring.

What about girls?

Oh, girls don't go to school.

That's not fair!

HIDDEN CITY

Your **lymphatic system** is a network of many different types of tissue that also cleanses and moves fluid. This is sort of an in-between system that supports both the circulatory and immune systems, which you learned about in Adventures 3 and 6.

If your blood vessels are like the roads in a city, the lymphatic system is like the plumbing underneath. The Aztecs built a city of waterways, using **aqueducts** to move water where it was needed and **canals** for transporting cargo and keeping the ancient metropolis clean.

Thoracic duct

Thymus Gland

Spleen

Right lymphatic duct

Tonsils

Lymph node

Using its very own pipelines, the lymphatic system has two very important jobs:
1) **balancing** the amount of fluid in your body, and
2) **filtering** that fluid to keep out harmful bacteria and viruses.

Chalchiuhtlicue

Here are the parts of your lymphatic system:

- **Lymph**, a clear, watery fluid made from old blood plasma, that carries cells, proteins, and fats through your entire body;
- **Lymph vessels**, tubes that collect and carry your lymph;
- **Spleen**, an organ that helps filter your blood;
- **Tonsils**, two fleshy masses in your throat, at the base of your tongue;
- **Thymus**, a gland behind your sternum that helps build immunity;
- **Peyer's patches**, in your small intestine, that monitor bacteria;
- **Lymph nodes**, home to your lymphocytes, or white blood cells.

Your lymph fluid is constantly moving through your body. As it flows through lymph vessels like water in the aqueducts of Tenochtitlan, lymph picks up all kinds of stuff—water, proteins, and of course, germs.

Some lymph goes directly back to your circulatory system, re-entering right before blood goes to the heart.

Lymph node

Red bone marrow

The rest drains to your lymph nodes, where lymphocytes look out for harmful invaders. Just like the water goddess Chalchiuhtlicue, lymphocytes are protectors.

Peyer's patches in intestinal wall

You have garbage men?

Sure! Tenochtitlan has everything a modern city needs.

Roads and canals to make travel easy.

Buildings where the work of the city gets done.

A system for disposing of waste.

We have limited entrances to the city center so we know who's coming in.

(Assuming they don't fall from the sky, like you girls.)

And people trained to defend the city from invaders.

No offense.

And the crown jewel of Tenochtitlan: the aqueduct!

This transports clean water from the lake all over the city.

This is all very impressive, but I'm afraid we're in a bit of a hurry.

Right! This is going to sound weird, but have you heard about a skeleton man around here?

I know exactly where we can find skeletons!

And something weird just happened there.

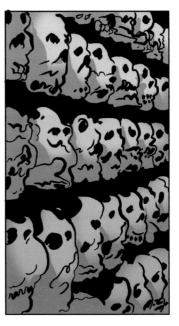

A Voyage Through Vessels & Valves

Part I: Look Before You Leak

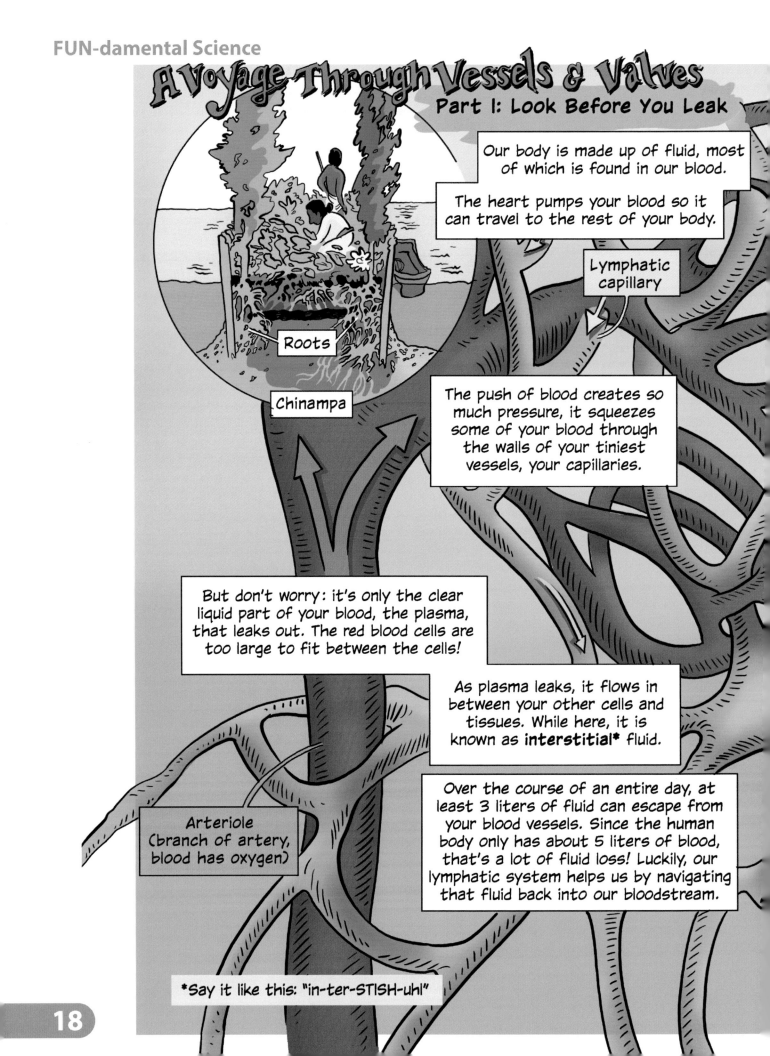

Roots

Chinampa

Lymphatic capillary

Arteriole
(branch of artery, blood has oxygen)

Our body is made up of fluid, most of which is found in our blood.

The heart pumps your blood so it can travel to the rest of your body.

The push of blood creates so much pressure, it squeezes some of your blood through the walls of your tiniest vessels, your capillaries.

But don't worry: it's only the clear liquid part of your blood, the plasma, that leaks out. The red blood cells are too large to fit between the cells!

As plasma leaks, it flows in between your other cells and tissues. While here, it is known as **interstitial** fluid.

Over the course of an entire day, at least 3 liters of fluid can escape from your blood vessels. Since the human body only has about 5 liters of blood, that's a lot of fluid loss! Luckily, our lymphatic system helps us by navigating that fluid back into our bloodstream.

*Say it like this: "in-ter-STISH-uhl"

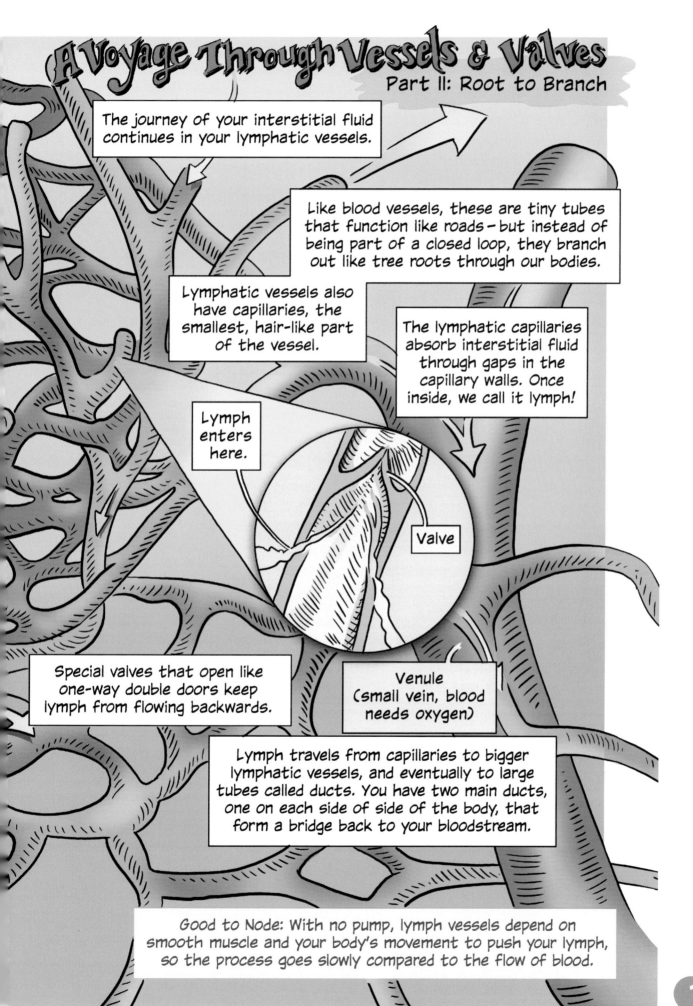

A Voyage Through Vessels & Valves

Part II: Root to Branch

The journey of your interstitial fluid continues in your lymphatic vessels.

Like blood vessels, these are tiny tubes that function like roads – but instead of being part of a closed loop, they branch out like tree roots through our bodies.

Lymphatic vessels also have capillaries, the smallest, hair-like part of the vessel.

The lymphatic capillaries absorb interstitial fluid through gaps in the capillary walls. Once inside, we call it lymph!

Lymph enters here.

Valve

Special valves that open like one-way double doors keep lymph from flowing backwards.

Venule (small vein, blood needs oxygen)

Lymph travels from capillaries to bigger lymphatic vessels, and eventually to large tubes called ducts. You have two main ducts, one on each side of side of the body, that form a bridge back to your bloodstream.

Good to Node: With no pump, lymph vessels depend on smooth muscle and your body's movement to push your lymph, so the process goes slowly compared to the flow of blood.

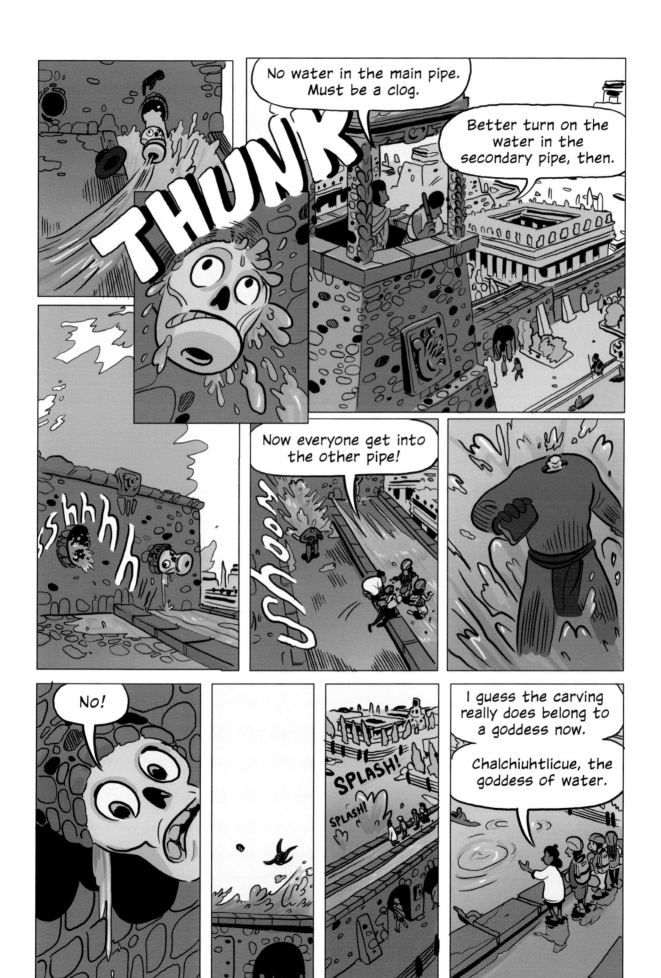

At least we have this rubbing. Hopefully, it will help us find Dr. B.

Hank, this says the Spanish are going to conquer Tenochtitlan in just a few decades!

Shouldn't we warn Monty?

No, that would violate the Core Protocol!

I have to agree with Naz on this.

We have no idea how warning Montezuma would affect the course of history.

Wow, did you guys go to the future again?

POP!

No, but it was kind of like an episode of Cosmic Voyager anyway.

I'll tell you all about it.

RRRRRUMMBBLE!! FFOOSH!!

Oh no.

NOTHING BUT NET

Before going back to the circulatory system, some of your lymph has one more stop – lymphatic tissues and organs!

Stomach

Spleen

Your **spleen** rests on your left side, behind the stomach, near the rib cage. A brown, flat oval, your spleen's primary function is to filter blood in the bloodstream.

Inside the spleen is a fiber structure that looks just like a spider web or a net.

When blood flows through the spleen, this net structure collects worn out red blood cells.

These red blood cells are recycled for their protein and iron nutrients.

The spleen also carries out an important waste collection process: gathering bacteria and sending them off to your **lymph nodes.**

Good to Node: Did you know you can live without a spleen? Since there are other organs that can filter blood, it is not a vital organ. However, people without a spleen sometimes do have a harder time healing.

NODE WARRIORS

Lymph nodes are bean-shaped structures that are very small, between 1 and 25 millimeters in length. You have 500-600 lymph nodes in your body. They are clustered together near your neck, armpits, chest, abdomen, and the crease of your hip.

Lymph nodes are home to your **lymphocytes**, also known as white blood cells. Many different cells in the body are lymphocytes, including thymus cells (i.e. T cells) and B cells. As you learned in Adventure 6, all lymphocytes act as your body's front line of protection.

Macrophage

When bacteria or other foreign invaders enter into your interstitial fluid, macrophages work the front lines. They can battle anything.

Tougher invaders move to the lymph nodes where B and T cells identify the type of invader, find the best counter-attack, then call for reinforcements. "Training" this specialized immunity makes B and T cells an effective army— against infection!

By acting as both a filter and protector, the lymphatic system supports the immune system to keep your body free of disease. It collects and inspects, and if needed – ejects!

T-Cell

Good to Node: Lymph nodes expand and enlarge during an invasion. By enlarging, the node gives your lymphocytes enough room to attack viruses, bacteria, and other foreign material.

Learning Calendar

Part 1

Know Your History

Estimated hours **5.5** hours of fun

Locate Mexico on the world map using a globe, an atlas, or an online map.

Read the comic Lymphin Large. Find it at the beginning of this Adventure Guide!

Gather the adventure equipment from around your house - use the checklist on pages 32-33.

Dig into *Know Your History*

Explore the paths *Where Water Winds* and **engineer** as an *Aztec Temple Tester*

Peruse *How the Gods Got Game,* and **score** when the *Ball's in Your Court*

Get your moves on in *Know Your Aztec Dance,* and **express yourself** in *Color Your Danza Azteca*

Get up-to-date with *Know Your Aztec Calendar,* and **travel through** *Take Time for a Spin*

Code your way through *Know Your Aztec Codex,* and **get creative** in *Long Story Short.*

Transcribe *Az-tec-hnically Speaking*

Analyze *Ancient Aztec Answers*

Part 2

Know Your Science

Get involved with *Know Your Lymphatic System*

Dive into *Know Your Spleen*

Deliver *Lymph Service*

Sort your way through *System Scramble*

Determine *whether To B Cell or Not to B Cell*

Merge everything together *with Movin' On Up*

Locate *The Lost Lymphocytes*

Piece together *Ex-SPLEEN What You Mean*

Part **3**

Know Your Appetite

Wander through *Explore Your Aztec Market*

Expose your taste buds *in Experience Mexican Cuisine*

Prepare *Mexican Hot Chocolate and Squash & Corn Tamales*

Share *your dishes with your family*

Discuss *Thoughts for Young Chefs around the table!*

Part **4**

Show What You Know!

Bring everything together *with Connect the Lymph Nodes*

Check out *Further Reading for more opportunities to learn.*

Great job on all your hard work!

Home Inventory Checklist

Ask your parents to help you find these items around the house. These are some of the tools you will need on your adventure.

- [ ] **Cardboard tubes (empty paper towel rolls or wrapping paper tubes)**
  - Where Water Winds
- [ ] **Cardboard boxes**
  - Where Water Winds
- [ ] **Plastic wrap or plastic sheeting**
  - Where Water Winds
- [ ] **Scissors**
  - Where Water Winds
- [ ] **Duct tape**
  - Where Water Winds
- [ ] **Balloon**
  - The Ball's in Your Court
- [ ] **2 Hula hoops (or cardboard boxes)**
  - The Ball's in Your Court
- [ ] **Masking tape or painter's tape**
  - The Ball's in Your Court
- [ ] **Shoebox**
  - Aztec Temple Tester
- [ ] **Liquid glue**
  - Aztec Temple Tester
- [ ] **Sugar cubes**
  - Aztec Temple Tester

- ☐ **Poster board**
  - Lymph Service
- ☐ **Markers, craft paint, or other materials**
  - Lymph Service
- ☐ **3 Empty liter bottles**
  - Lymph Service
- ☐ **Water**
  - Lymph Service
- ☐ **Optional: Yarn, beads, glue**
  - To B Cell or Not to B Cell
- ☐ **Four 3" by 5" note cards**
  - To B Cell or Not to B Cell
- ☐ **Chess or checkers board**
  - To B Cell or Not to B Cell
- ☐ **Pen or pencil**
  - To B Cell or Not to B Cell

Check the items off when you've found them!

Be creative if you don't have something on the list.

Tenochtitlan: City of Marvels

In 1325, on the site of present-day Mexico City, the Aztecs started building a great metropolis called **Tenochtitlan*** on a small island in Lake Texcoco. They chose the location based on a sign from the gods. The sign was an **eagle perched on a cactus with a snake in its beak**. At its height, the city boasted huge stone temples and palaces, canals, fresh running water, and a royal zoo.

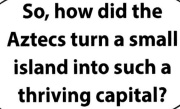

So, how did the Aztecs turn a small island into such a thriving capital?

Chinampas

The Aztecs extended the small island by creating more islands called **Chinampas***. These are like floating gardens. First, they sank wooden boards into the lake. Then, they filled in the area between the boards with mud, rocks, and reeds. In this way, they expanded their city until it covered five square miles.

Spanish conquistador, Hernán Cortés, landed in Mexico in 1519. By that time, the Chinampas provided food for a population of 5 to 6 million people! Their aqueducts carried fresh water for drinking and watering crops. Their agricultural system is considered a marvel of its time.

Roots

Chinampa

*Say them like this:

tenochtitlan - "teh-knowch-**TEET**-lawn"
chinampas - "chee-**NAHM**-pa"

The strongest syllable is always shown in **CAPITALS** and **red**.

Montezuma* II

Montezuma II was a **great warrior** and the ninth ruler of Tenochtitlan, from 1501 to 1519. This city was probably larger than any capital in western Europe at the time. Montezuma's empire stretched from the Pacific Ocean to the Gulf of Mexico.

*Say them like this:

montezuma - "mont-uh-**ZOOM**-a"   **nahuatl** - "**NAH**-waht"

The strongest syllable is always shown in **CAPITALS** and **red**.

His people were educated and spoke a complex language called **Nahuatl*** and used advanced math. His palace had **hanging gardens, pools, and a private zoo** with hundreds of **exotic animals**. Three thousand servants cared for him. He ate on special pottery behind a gold screen, entertained by jugglers and acrobats. He was fascinated with the arts, philosophy, and astrology.

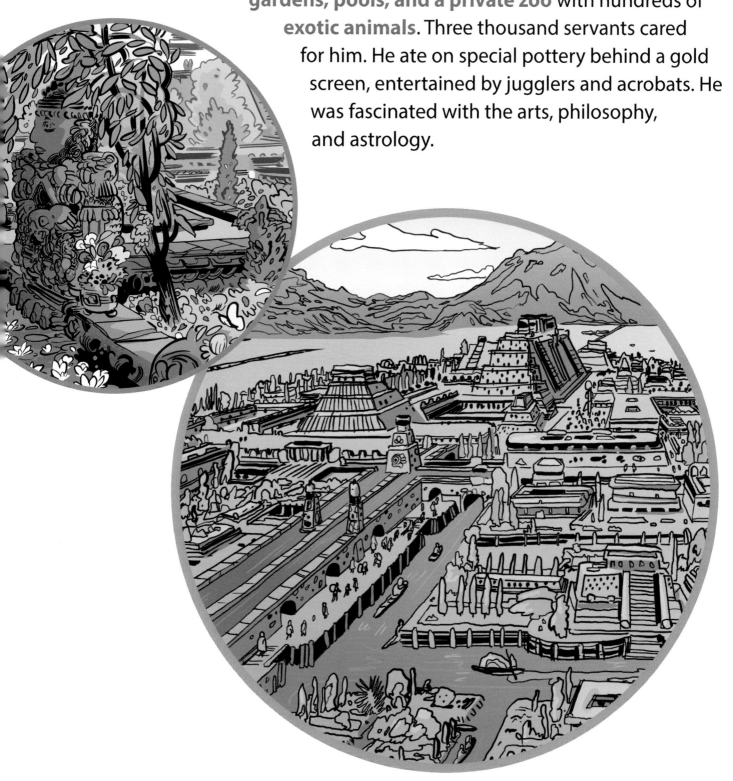

Where Water Winds

The water under the city of Tenochtitlan was not suitable for drinking or cooking, so the Aztec people needed to find a solution as the city grew. The water in the nearby Chapultepec springs was fresh and drinkable, but too far away to travel every time they needed a drink. They came up with a solution to make gravity do all the work: an aqueduct, or water bridge. This large structure carried water about **2.5 miles** from the springs to the city, where it could be redirected to the people who needed it. While aqueducts have been largely replaced with pipes today, they were important to the growth of most ancient cities across the world.

coloring
opportunity

Build Your Own Aqueduct

Materials:

- **Cardboard tube**
- **Cardboard boxes**
- **Plastic wrap or plastic sheeting**
- **Scissors**
- **Duct Tape**

Directions:

1. Cut your cardboard tubes in half lengthwise, to create a long U-shape. Use tape to connect the two halves to extend the tube if it is shorter.

2. Starting at the end, wrap the plastic so that it covers the inside of the U and just goes over the edge. Tape it down tight. That will be the bottom of your aquaduct.

   - Repeat as needed moving up the tube, ensuring that each new plastic section overlaps the previous one.

3. Using your cardboard boxes, construct supports for the tube using these instructions:

- Cut out two matching triangular pieces at the height you want your tube to start.

- Cut out a rectangular piece approximately twice the width of your tube and the length of your triangle bottoms.

- Tape the bottoms of the triangles to the rectangular piece, and the top of the triangles to either side of the end of the tube.

- Repeat this process for every few inches of the tube, with the triangles 1" lower each time.

4. Place your aqueduct somewhere that the water can safely pour and add water slowly on the taller end to watch it travel with just the aid of gravity.

Aztec Temple Tester

Pyramids were made using stone blocks, formed from natural materials such as wood, rocks, mud, and limestone. One popular pyramid style looked like a long staircase on four sides and had a temple on top. The Aztecs built large pyramids and temples for religious reasons. Temples were placed at the very top of these tall pyramids because the Aztecs believed that to be closest to where the gods lived. In the temples, you can find pictures or shrines that honor a god in Aztec culture.

Build your own Aztec Temple

Put your Aztec temple building skills to the test using the materials and directions below

Needed:

- **Shoebox**
- **Liquid glue**
- **Sugar cubes**

Directions:

1. Take the top from an empty shoebox and lay it flat on a table surface. This will be used as the ground for your pyramid.

2. Create a glue layer to hold down the base of your pyramid. Then place 64 sugar cubes into a square shape (8 x 8 cubes) on top of the glue.

3. Make it look like a staircase by using 49 sugar cubes for your next square layer (7 x 7 cubes) - setting a layer of glue in between each new set of sugar cubes.

4. Repeat step 3 but use 36 sugar cubes (6 x 6 cubes). Then continue the stair pattern with 25 sugar cubes (5 x 5 cubes), 16 sugar cubes (4 x 4 cubes), 9 sugar cubes (3 x 3 cubes), 4 sugar cubes (2 x 2 cubes), until you get to 1 sugar cube.

* If you would like more of a challenge, see if you can make the inside of the pyramid hollow. You may need a few more materials you may have around the house to do so.

The Gods Got Game

A popular ball game played among the Aztec civilization was **ULLAMALIZTLI.***

Probably only for nobles, the game was played on a long, narrow court called a **TLACHTLI.*** It had high walls, shaped like the letter "I" and a small, stone ring hung on each end. The walls were often very decorative, and these courts were a great source of pride.

During game play, two teams faced each other across a line in the middle of the court. The object was to get a rubber ball through the ring on the other team's side. It was a bit like basketball, except players could only touch the ball with their elbows, knees, and hips! They threw themselves on the ground to hit the ball with only those parts of their bodies.

Besides being fun and physically challenging, ullamaliztli had a religious meaning. Games were considered contests between the god of the sun and god of the moon, with each of the two teams playing on one god's behalf. The Aztecs also believed the court represented the world and the ball a star or planet. Because of this, they built the courts near the most important temples, like the Great Temple in Tenochtitlan.

Let's set up your own modern day version of ullamaliztli!

*Say them like this:

ullamaliztli - "oo-la-ma-**LEETZ**-lee"   **tlachtli** - "**tlach**-tlee"

The strongest syllable is always shown in **CAPITALS** and **red.**

The Ball's in Your Court

Materials

- **A balloon**
- **An open space like a large room or your backyard**

    (where there isn't anything to break!)

- **Something to be your goal such as**

    1) a small hula hoop, or

    2) a cardboard box with both ends open, to form a square hoop.

    You'll need one for each team.

- **Masking or blue painter's tape**

    (something that won't leave marks on the wall)

- **2–4 players**
- **Pen**

The Balls in Your Court

Directions:

1. Secure your hula hoops or boxes against a wall so they are accessible from both ends. The goals should be at least waist-height.

2. Practice the basic moves

- Hold the balloon in front of you; drop it as you bring your knee up and bump it into the air.

- Try to bump the balloon with your hip.

- While turning your waist, try to bump the balloon with your elbow (try clasping hand-over-hand, so you use your whole body, not just your arm).

3. Try the moves with a friend. Can you pass the balloon to each other?

4. Now try passing the balloon between three other friends. It's more challenging!

5. Once you feel comfortable passing, divide into teams and try to get the balloon through your team's hoop! Play for 20 minutes and see who can score the most points.

No matter who wins, remember to have fun! Enjoy the game!

Danza Azteca

The Aztecs worshiped their gods through **dance.** A dance began with a circle of people turning silently in each direction: north, south, east and west. This was followed by drumming, loud and strong enough to be felt in the whole body.

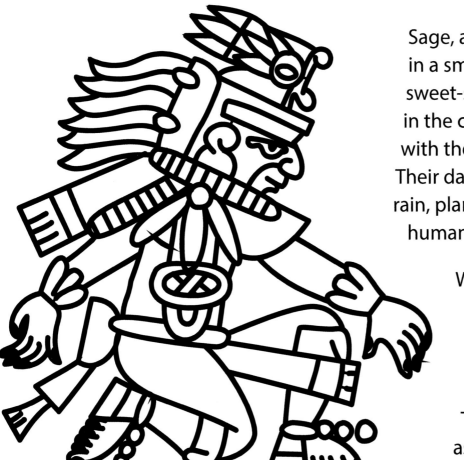

Sage, a dried herb, was burned in a small stone bowl to make a sweet-smelling smoke. The feeling in the circle was powerful, filled with the energy of the dancers. Their dance honored nature, the sun, rain, plants, and animals as one with humankind.

While we don't know the exact date of the origin of **Danza Azteca**, we do know that it came before **Cuauhtemoc*** (the last Aztec emperor). This ritual dance was known as **Macehualiztli,*** meaning "deserving" in the Aztec language of Nahuatl.

* Say them like this:
cuauhtémoc - "kwa-TEH-mock"
macehualiztli - "mah-keh-wa-LEETZ-lee"
The strongest syllable is always shown in **CAPITALS** and **red**.

The dance represented their eternal search for harmony with the universe, as well as the integration of body and spirit. Danza Azteca was a way of life and communication with the Aztec gods, which were very important to the Aztec people. The dancers (dazante) moved together as one, stepping and jumping in unison. This meditative dance helped the Aztecs feel more connected to their gods. Like prayer, their movement was a form of spiritual ceremony.

As a danzante Azteca, there is a lot of sweating and ridding of toxins! In this Adventure, you learned that the lymphatic system's job is to rid the body of germs and waste. Since this system does not have a pump, your lymphatic vessels rely on your skeletal muscle to push lymph as you move.

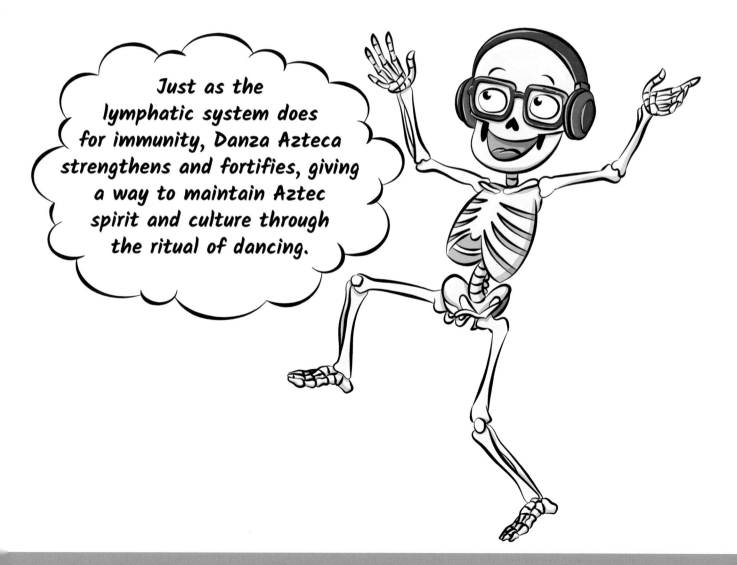

Just as the lymphatic system does for immunity, Danza Azteca strengthens and fortifies, giving a way to maintain Aztec spirit and culture through the ritual of dancing.

Color Your Danza

coloring
opportunity

Know Your

Aztec Calendar

About 500 years ago, the Aztec people created a giant calendar called the Sun Stone to illustrate their view of the world. This was not just any calendar, it was carved into a slab of solid rock, 12 feet across, that weighed as much as a small whale. Nobody even knew the amazing stone existed until it was found buried in Mexico in 1790!

Although you'll notice some similarities, the Aztec calendar tracked days, months, and years very differently than a modern calendar. Plus, there are actually two calendars—the **Xiuhpohualli*** and the **Tonalpohualli***—which were used for different purposes. With the combination of the two, no date was ever repeated for 18,980 days. That's 52 years!

Think of the Tonalpohualli calendar as two wheels. The first day of the 260-day cycle begins with the small wheel set at number 1 and the middle wheel set to the cipactli or crocodile symbol.

The second day of the year combines the number 2 with the enecatl or wind symbol. You can try this out on the next page with your own Tonalpohualli calendar!

Know Your Aztec Calendar

The Xiuhpohualli* calendar was solar (based on the movement of the sun) and contained 365 days. It had 18 separate "months" of 20 days each, called **veintenas,*** plus 5 extra "unlucky" days. The calendar showed the cycle of the four seasons and helped the Aztecs decide when to plant crops and plan for the future.

The Tonalpohualli*, or "day counting," calendar was the Aztec ritual calendar and contained 260 days. Time was broken into 20 different "months" of 13 days each, called **trecenas.*** A day was marked by a number and a symbol, or daysign. Examples of some daysigns are cipactli (crocodile), ehecatl (wind), and calli (house). To keep everything in balance throughout the year, a different deity was assigned to each trecena.

---

*Say them like this:

xiuhpohualli - "shu-pa-**WA**-le"   **tonalpohualli -** "tone-all-pa-**WA**-lee"
veintenas - "bane-**TEH**-nuhz"   **trecenas -** "treh-**SEH**-nuhz"

The strongest syllable is always shown in **CAPITALS** and **red**.

Bonus Challenge:
Can you guess which words are Nahuatl and which are Spanish?

_____

NAHUATL: _____

SPANISH: _____

After you finish, check the answer key on page 113

Assemble Your

Aztec Calendar

Materials:

- **Aztec Calendar Printouts (pages 54-57)**

- **Brad or thumbtack**

- **Four pieces of cardboard the same size as each printout**

- **Paperclip and/or Brad**

- **Glue**

Directions:

1. Cut out each calendar printout to remove the white on the outside of the ring. Leave the centers intact.

2. Cut out a piece of cardboard the same size as each of the three circles you have.

3. Glue each calendar piece to the matching piece of cardboard. Wait for the glue to dry before you continue. Your calendar won't work if it gets stuck together!

4. Using your paper-clip, poke a hole through each piece in the center of the circle.

5. Use a brad to connect all four pieces together through the center hole. (You can use the paper-clip if you don't have a brad.)

6. Make sure that all the pieces can move independently of one another before you finish securing the calendar.

You're now ready to try your calendar!

Aztec Calendar Printable

Aztec Calendar

Cut here

Card
A

circle #2

Cut here

circle #1

KNOW
YOURSELF

Aztec Calendar Printable

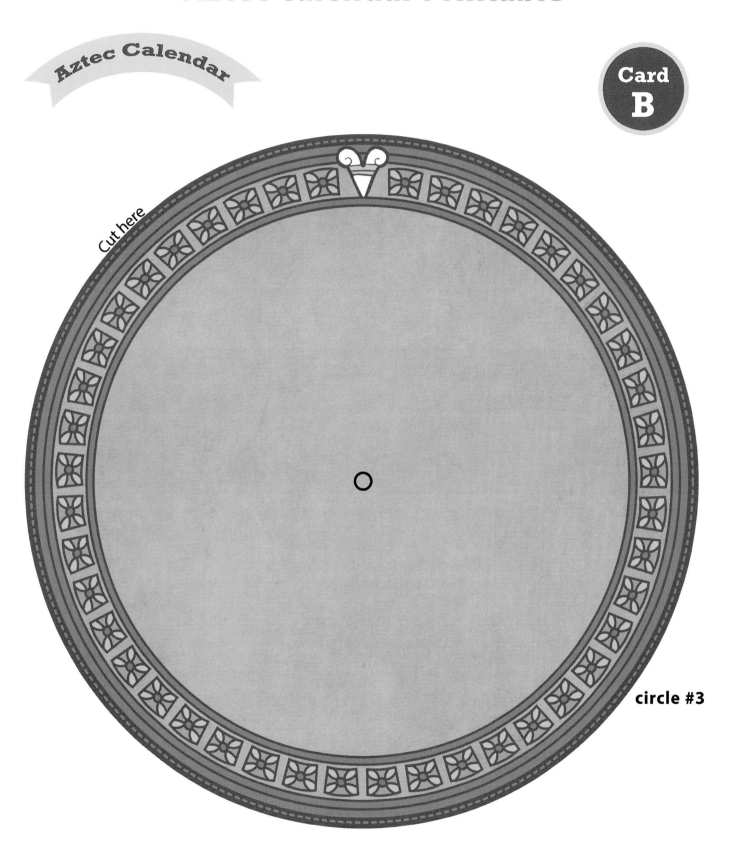

Aztec Calendar

Cut here

circle #3

Aztec Calendar Printable

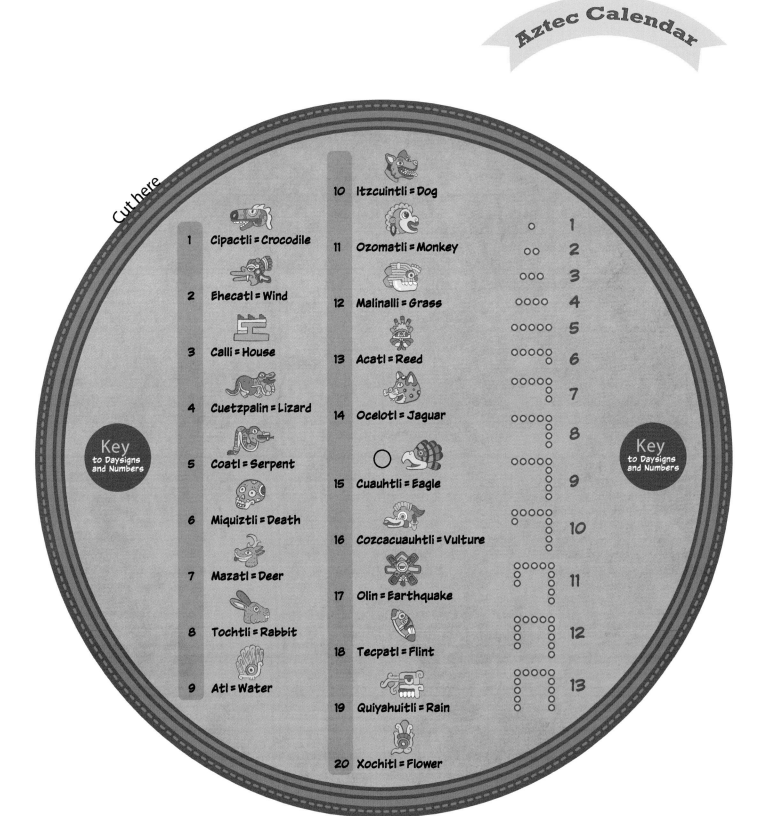

Cut here

Key
to Daysigns
and Numbers

1 Cipactli = Crocodile

2 Ehecatl = Wind

3 Calli = House

4 Cuetzpalin = Lizard

5 Coatl = Serpent

6 Miquiztli = Death

7 Mazatl = Deer

8 Tochtli = Rabbit

9 Atl = Water

10 Itzcuintli = Dog

11 Ozomatli = Monkey

12 Malinalli = Grass

13 Acatl = Reed

14 Ocelotl = Jaguar

15 Cuauhtli = Eagle

16 Cozcacuauhtli = Vulture

17 Olin = Earthquake

18 Tecpatl = Flint

19 Quiyahuitli = Rain

20 Xochitl = Flower

Key
to Daysigns
and Numbers

○ 1

○○ 2

○○○ 3

○○○○ 4

○○○○○ 5

○○○○○○ 6

○○○○○○○ 7

8

9

10

11

12

13

circle #4

Take Time for a Spin Printable

Trecenas	Deity
1 Crocodile to 13 Reed	Ometeotl
1 Jaguar to 13 Death	Quetzalcoatl
1 Deer to 13 Rain	Tepeyollotl
1 flower to 13 Grass	Huehuecoyotl
1 Reed to 13 Snake	Chalchiuhtlicue
1 Death to 13 Flint	Tonatiuh
1 Rain to 13 Monkey	Tlaloc
1 Grass to 13 Lizard	Mayahuel
1 Snake to 13 Quake	Xiuhtecuhtli
1 Flint to 13 Dog	Mictlantecuhtli
1 Monkey to 13 House	Patecatl
1 Lizard to 3 Vulture	Itztlacoliuhqui
1 Quake to 13 Water	Tlazolteotl
1 Dog to 13 Wind	Xipe Totec
1 House to 13 Eagle	Itzpapalotl
1 Vulture to 13 Rabbit	Xolotl
1 Water to 13 Crocodile	Chalchiuhtotolin
1 Wind to 13 Jaguar	Chantico
1 Eagle to 13 Deer	Xochiquetzal
1 Rabbit to 13 Flower	Xiuhtecuhtli

Take Time for a Spin

Materials:

- **Your assembled Aztec Calendar with Key (page 57)**

Directions:

1. Get familiar with the Key on the back of your calendar.

2. Find the arrow on the outer edge of the front of the large circle and position it at the top. This is where you will align the numbers and daysigns as you move through a trecena (*aztec months*).

3. Align the crocodile (on the middle circle) and the symbol for number (on the small circle) with the arrow. This is day one of your trecena and this combination is called "1 Crocodile."

4. Moving counterclockwise, align the symbol for number 2 and the symbol for wind with the arrow. This is day two of your trecena and is called "2 Wind."

5. Move through all 13 days of the trecena until you are back to number 1 on the small circle and day sign 14 on the middle circle. This is the beginning of the second trecena.

6. Using the key on the previous page, can you figure out which deity governs the third trecena? What about the tenth?

coloring
opportunity

Know Your Aztec Codex

Hey, That Looks Like a Comic Book!

Aztec society was enormously complex, with an advanced command of economy, arts, and science unlike much of the world had ever seen. They even had their very own version of a comic book called a codex (plural: codices).

The spiral-shaped speech scroll was used to indicate the idea of speech.

An Aztec codex is basically a story told with pictures, much like Egyptian hieroglyphics. Images are strung together to depict **narratives***, from explanations of the Aztec calendar to descriptions of deities.

Codices were created long before the Spanish conquest. Often made from strips of deer hide, cotton cloth, or bark paper, a codex was folded accordion style and could sometimes be 40 feet long! The Aztecs painted with bright red, yellow, blue, and green, using materials like flowers, fruit, even insects!

Many cultures, from the Aztecs to the Egyptians, have historically used symbols to tell stories. In some ways, they are similar to illustrated story books. They are like comics from the ancient world.

It's your turn to be a **tlacuilo!*** Also known as scribes, tlacuilos were specially trained to paint codices. Thanks to their work, we have been able to learn about the Aztecs and their way of life.
Now, you're going to create your very own codex.

What kinds of stories will you tell?

If you like emojis or stickers, you know how much fun it can be to reply with an image. Challenge yourself to tell a story with your "Know Yourself Picture" images!

> * Say them like this:
>
> **tlacuilo - "tlah-KWEE-low" narrative - "NAIR-uh-tiv"**
>
> The strongest syllable is always shown in **CAPITALS** and **red**.

Printable Picture Page - Long Story Short

Long Story Short

Create your codex

To create your codex, first look at the pictures on your printed picture pages. How can you use these to show character, setting, and action? A picture can have meanings in a different way than words.

Materials:

- **Printed picture page**

- **Scissors**

- **Paper grocery bag**

- **Markers or colored pencils**

- **Gluestick or tape**

Directions:

1. Take your paper bag and cut it so that you end up with one large rectangular piece of paper.

2. Holding your paper, fold the longest length in half, and then fold it the same way. Fold it one more time if you can. It should unfold like an accordion to make the shape on the previous page.

3. Ask yourself: who is in your story? What discovery are they making, or what problem are they trying to solve? Each panel will show a section of your narrative (*another word for story*).

4. Panels separate points in time–from moments to years apart. Think about how you will show the passage of time.

5. Cut out any pictures you want from the Picture Page printout and use a gluestick or tape to attach them to the panels where they should be. Use your markers or colored pencils to draw your own additions.

Your imagination is the only limit!

Aztec-nically Speaking

After you finish, check the answer key on page 110.

Across:

4. Floating islands made from wooden boards, mud, rocks, and reeds

6. An agricultural marvel used for moving fresh water

7. Buyers and sellers who traveled the Aztec trade routes

9. Known as the City of Marvels

Down:

1. The last name of a Spanish conquistador

2. This means "Welcome" in Nahuatl

3. The language of the ancient Aztec

5. Ruled Mexico's capital city from 1501 to 1519

8. The bean used as Aztec currency

10. A place where Aztecs honor the gods

Ancient Aztec Answers

Good work Adventurers!

Now that you have read some things about Ancient Mexico, let's review what you have learned!

Fill in the blanks below

The Aztecs started building their capital __ __ __ __ __ __ __ __ __ __ __ __

in 1325. While the location started as a small island, they expanded it with

__ __ __ __ __ __ __ __ __, a type of floating garden. At its height the city was

__ __ __ __ square miles and had a population of over __ __ __ __ million. One of

the most impressive engineering accomplishments carried fresh water for people

to drink and to water crops called an __ __ __ __ __ __ __ __.

The ninth ruler of Tenochtitlan was named __ __ __ __ __ __ __ __ __ __ __ __. The

Aztec Empire under him stretched from the __ __ __ __ __ __ __ ocean to the

Gulf of __ __ __ __ __ __. The palace contained hanging __ __ __ __ __ __ __ __,

pools and even a private __ __ __.

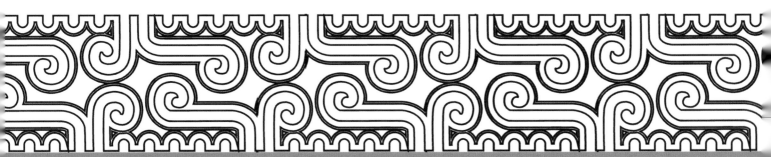

Many of these accomplishments were possible because of the advanced

__ __ __ __ used by the Atzec people. The Aztecs used a massive calendar

called the __ __ __ __ __ __ __ which was carved into solid __ __ __ __. This

combined two systems, the Xiuhpohualli which tracked the __ __ __ and the Ton-

alpohualli which counted __ __ __ __. These two combined to create the Aztec

calendar, which wouldn't repeat a date for __ __ __ __ __-__ __ __ years.

After you finish, check the answer key on page 111.

coloring
opportunity

Know Your Lymphatic System

Cleaning House

Your circulatory system and immune system can't do their jobs on their own. They need the body's unsung hero: the lymphatic system.

This system helps maintain your blood pressure and serves as the body's first line of defense, seeking and destroying foreign invaders like viruses and bacteria.

YOUR LYMPHATIC SYSTEM HAS FIVE KEY COMPONENTS:

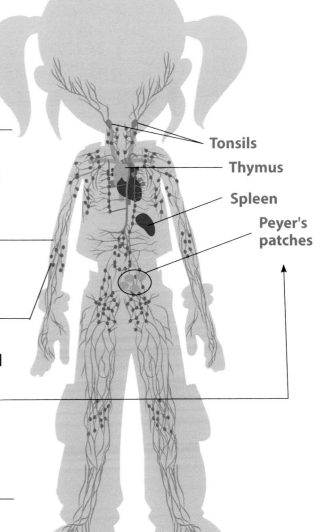

Tonsils

Thymus

Spleen

Peyer's patches

1 **Lymph**—the fluid that travels through your lymphatic system.

2 **Lymphatic Vessels**—a lot like your blood vessels, but they carry lymph instead of blood. Think of them as a big aqueduct for lymph fluid.

3 **Lymph Nodes**—checkpoints that filter your lymph and check for viruses and bacteria.

4 **Lymph Organs**—your tonsils, thymus, spleen, and Peyer's patches perform special functions to protect your body.

5 **Lymphocytes**—white blood Cells that live in the lymphatic tissue. They're your body's guardians and deal with harmful foreign invaders.

Blood travels through your body via thin blood vessels called capillaries. As it pushes through these capillaries, the pressure inside forces some of the blood's clear fluid, called plasma, to leak out.

Don't worry, this is normal! Most of this fluid goes back to your blood vessels, but each day, three whole liters of fluid get left behind. Your lymph vessels collect that fluid—now called lymph—and start it on the journey back to the bloodstream.

And you need that fluid! Your body requires roughly five liters of blood in circulation to function properly. If your lymphatic system didn't return that fluid to your bloodstream, eventually your blood pressure would drop so low that you would die. That's why the lymphatic system works both to maintain the fluid balance in your body and filter your blood.

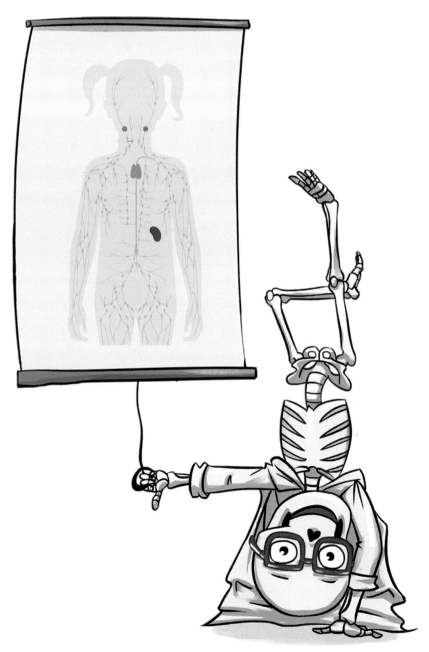

Know Your Lymphatic System

After traveling through the lymphatic vessels and a series of nodes, your lymph passes through one of two ducts, which serve as bridges between your lymphatic vessels and your bloodstream.

The fluid collected from your right arm, the right side of your chest, neck, and head ends up in the right lymphatic duct. The fluid from the rest of your body drains into the thoracic duct (left lymphatic duct). Here it enters the bloodstream, just before it goes back to the heart.

The lymphatic system works to maintain both the fluid balance in your body and filter your blood.

Node Diggity

While your lymph travels through the lymph nodes, lymphocytes search for foreign invaders, such as bacteria and viruses, that have come along for the ride. In some cases, the lymphocyte can easily destroy invaders on its own. When it needs help, the lymphocyte tags the invader, telling the immune system to destroy it.

Every now and then, a lymph node finds itself overwhelmed by these invaders and swells up. You might notice that when you have a cold or other infection, you or your doctor can feel little bumps near your throat. Those bumps are swollen lymph nodes, which mean your lymphocytes are hard at work fighting off invading Cells.

Good to Node:
When your lymphatic system is not working efficiently, **edema*** might occur. This is when **interstitial*** fluid, the fluid that sits between your body's tissues, builds up and causes swelling–especially in your legs, feet, or hands. "Edema" comes from the Greek oidema, which means "swelling."

* Say them like this:

edema - "eh-DEE-muh"
interstitial - "in-ter-STISH-uhl"

The strongest syllable is always shown in **CAPITALS** and **red**.

Know Your Spleen

In your comic, your spleen is described as a net. To be more exact, it's like a net with pockets of liquid. Think of the structure of an orange or similar fruit.

The spleen is in a **capsule**, a thick coating of connective tissue that encases the organ. This capsule can expand, letting the spleen fill with blood, or contract, forcing blood back out again. Inside, you'll find two kinds of tissue: **white pulp**, which is typically found around the spleen's blood vessels, and **red pulp**. Just like the pulp of an orange is filled with tiny pockets of juice, your spleen's red pulp is filled with tiny pockets of blood.

Spleen

The white pulp contains areas called **germinal centers**, where lymphocytes, the lymphatic system's guardians, are produced. Your lymph nodes also have these germinal centers and produce lymphocytes of their own.

Your blood is filtered through the red pulp. That's where worn out red blood cells are recycled. The red pulp also contains large quantities of special white blood cells known as **monocytes**, which help serve another important function. When a part of the body gets hurt, the spleen releases monocytes, which travel to the site of the injury and help it heal. Although you *can* live without your spleen, it's still a valuable organ when it comes to keeping your body healthy.

In addition to your spleen, there are other organs that dispose of red blood cells. Your liver is mostly responsible for breaking down old red blood cells and recycling the iron and proteins.

LYMPH AND LEARN

Lymph is about 95 percent water.

The word lymph comes from the name of the Roman deity for fresh water, Lympha.

Because they're so small, lymph nodes are considered to be tissues, not organs. They range in size from 1 to 25 millimeters.

Tonsil

Thymus Gland

Lymph Nodes

Subclavian Vein

Thoracic Duct

Heart

Spleen

Tonsils are large clusters of lymphatic cells.

Some animals have tonsils, too. Dogs, rabbits, and goats each have six!

Did you know you could be born with more than one spleen? Many organs come in pairs, but usually people have only one spleen.

Lymph Nodes

Lymphatic Vessels

Lymph Service

Materials:

- **Poster Board**

- **Markers, craft paint, or other materials**

- **3 empty liter bottles**

- **Water**

- **Optional: Yarn, beads, glue**

Directions:

1. Start by laying your poster board flat on the floor. Ask a friend to help you trace your body, from your neck to your hip area, on the poster board.

2. Fill in the poster version of you with your Lymphatic System components: *lymph, lymphatic vessels, lymph nodes, lymph organs (the tonsils, thymus, spleen, and peyer's patches), and lymphocytes.* Use the diagram located in Know Your Lymphatic System to help you place your parts.

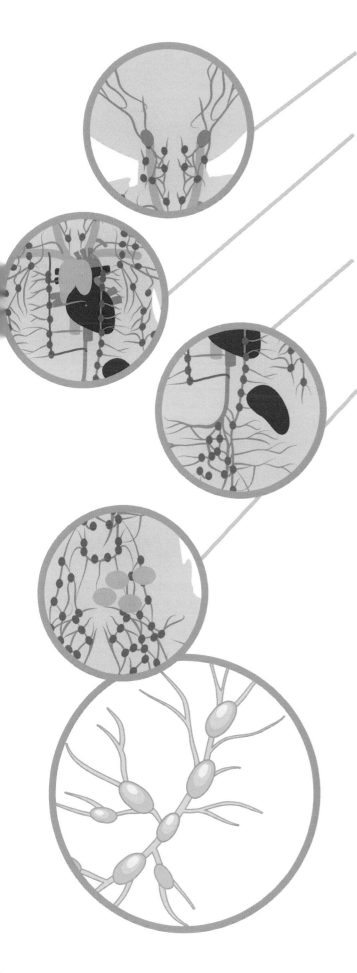

3. Paint your tonsils on each side of the back of your throat.

4. Paint your thymus. Your thymus can be compared to a pair of butterfly wings and is located in front of your heart.

5. Draw in your spleen behind your left ribs and near your stomach. From a back angle, it might look sort of like a clenched fist.

6. Add in your peyer patches, which appear round or oval in shape and are stationed in the lining of your small intestine.

7. Once you are finished illustrating the lymphatic system organs, design lymphatic vessels and lymph nodes using your markers. Draw lines to represent vessels and circles to represent nodes. If you want to be extra crafty, try using yarn for vessels and beads for nodes (you'll need some liquid glue to hold things in place).

Bonus:

To imagine how much lymph is floating around your whole body at one time, take your 3 empty liter bottles and fill them to the top with water. Now set those next to your diagram.

Your Lymphatic System

Oh No!

The lymphatic system names were scrambled and we need your help filling in the blanks.

Unscramble the words below.

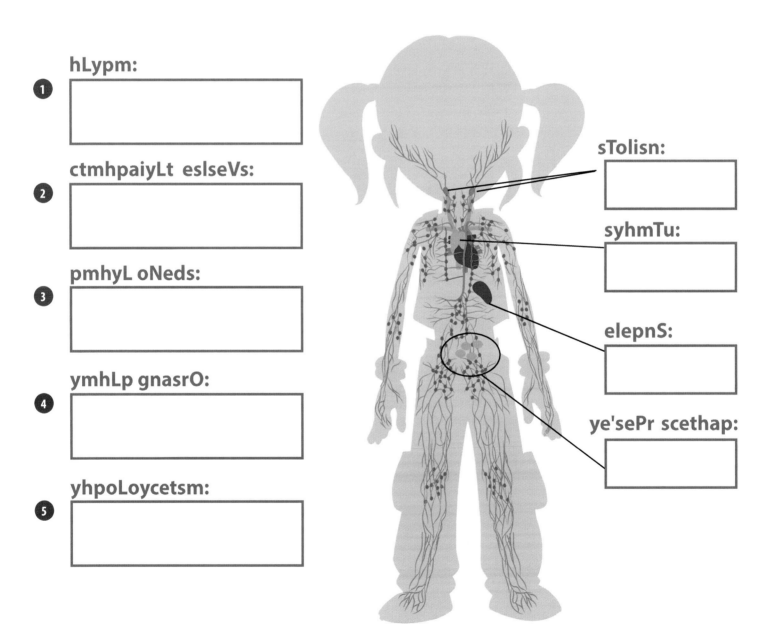

hLypm:

① _____

ctmhpaiyLt eslseVs:

② _____

pmhyL oNeds:

③ _____

ymhLp gnasrO:

④ _____

yhpoLoycetsm:

⑤ _____

sTolisn:
_____

syhmTu:
_____

elepnS:
_____

ye'sePr scethap:
_____

After you finish, check the answer key on page 114.

To B-Cell or Not to B-Cell

Materials:

- **Four 3" by 5" note cards**
- **Chess or checkers board**
- **Pen or pencil**
- **A second player for the game**

Directions:

1. Cut each note card in half lengthwise. Afterwards, you will have eight 1.5" by 5" cards.

2. Carefully cut each of the eight pieces into five more pieces (1.5" by 1"). You should now have 40 1" by 1.5" pieces that look the same. It's important to make sure you can't tell them apart.

3. Fold all of them in half so they stand up on their own.

4. Decide which 32 look the most identical. Then, mark them on one side only.

5. For all the markings, it shouldn't be possible to tell what it says when looking from the other side.

    - Mark 16 of them with an "N" or "Normal"
    - Mark 4 "B Cell"
    - Mark 4 "Helper T Cell"
    - Mark 4 "Bacteria"
    - Mark 4 "Virus"
    - Any that you set aside as being unusual should be marked "Virus" also.

6. Get your game board and get ready to play.

Play

1. One player is playing as the Lymphatic system. Give them eight normal cells, the B cells, and the Helper T cells.

2. The other player is playing as 'Disease'; give them eight normal cells, the bacteria and four of the virus infected cells. Set the rest of the virus cards aside, they will be used later.

3. Have each player set up their cells in the first three rows of the board closest to them, organizing however they would like. Keep the markings of each piece a secret.

4. The disease player goes first.

5. On each turn, a player can move a piece one space in any direction. They can't move into a space with a piece they control. If they move onto a space with a piece controlled by the other player, reveal both pieces and consult the chart to see what happens, then go to the next player.

6. If a normal cell has been placed flat, it can't be moved anymore.

7. Play continues until either all the bacteria and viruses have been eliminated or captured, or until all the B or Helper T cells have been eliminated.

TARGET CELL

MOVING CELL	Normal	B Cell	Helper T	Bacteria	Virus
Normal	Reveal both and place flat	Nothing happens	Nothing happens	Remove Normal	Remove Normal
B Cell	Reveal normal and place flat	-	-	Capture	Capture
Helper T	Nothing happens	Special	-	Remove Helper T	Remove Helper T
Bacteria	Remove Normal	Capture Remove	Remove Helper T	-	-
Virus	Replace normal with virus	Capture or Remove	Remove Helper T	-	-

When a B cell captures a bacteria or virus, place the B cell on top of the captured piece. A B cell that has captured a cell can no longer be moved.

If a Helper T cell moves into a space with a B cell that has captured a bacteria or virus, all of the captured piece types are removed from the game as antibodies are produced. (For example, all Bacteria are removed if a bacteria was captured.)

If a bacteria or virus moves onto a B cell, it is captured unless that B cell has already captured a bacteria or virus. If it captured the same type of disease cell, then nothing happens. If a bacteria moves onto a B cell that captured a virus or vice versa, the B cell and the captured cell are destroyed together.

Movin' On Up

Where anatomy, physiology, and psychology all come together

The circulatory system has the heart to pump blood through your body, but the lymphatic system does not have a pump at all! How do our bodies get our lymph to travel?

Follow the Path!

Sometimes we get sick, but we almost always get better because the body's "army" fights off germs. As lymph flows, it carries foreign invaders to our warrior lymphocytes. They attack bad bacteria and viruses that can cause colds and infections. Remember how muscle contracts from Adventure 7? As we move, muscles squeeze lymphatic vessels and our lymph moves on up!

In addition to our skeletal muscles (the muscles in your legs, for example), other body parts help get your lymph moving. Nearby arteries pulse as blood flows! Smooth muscle in the walls of your lymphatic vessels contracts rhythmically! It's almost like a big dance party, where one person starts dancing and soon so is everyone else.

Lymph that flows well means clean blood, germ control, and a healthier you. You feel brighter, more uplifted, and ready to move forward. When you get moving, your lymph does too. Sometimes we get sick, but we almost always get better because the body's "army" fights off germs.

"Move forward," "Look ahead," or
"Don't look back" are often said as encouragement.

What else does the phrase,
"Moving forward" mean to you?

Follow Pinky and get your muscles to move your lymph:

1. Rotate your head to move lymph through the neck nodes.

2. Shrug your shoulders like you're saying "Huh?" Release like you're saying "Uh-huh."

3. Twist your waist and let your arms swing around like a pinwheel.

4. March in place like a high stepper!

5. Lift your arms like you're aiming a basketball at a hoop

6. Jump up and take your shot!

Locate Lost Lymphocytes

LYMPH   BALANCE   TONSILS

VESSELS   DUCTS   THYMUS

NODES   BACTERIA   SPLEEN

EDEMA   VIRUS   PEYERS

INTERSTITIAL   GERMINAL

CAPSULE

```
I  G  Y  S  P  L  E  E  N  F  L  C  Q  H  T
B  N  D  N  A  U  K  L  Y  M  P  H  U  T  Y
V  A  T  V  I  R  U  S  H  S  H  Q  R  H  G
E  X  L  E  T  C  Z  S  E  H  G  W  B  Y  E
S  C  P  A  R  B  A  C  T  E  R  I  A  M  R
S  X  A  E  N  S  P  M  M  T  C  N  S  U  M
E  P  M  P  Y  C  T  E  Z  G  N  P  B  S  I
L  Z  W  F  S  E  E  I  D  J  K  O  T  Z  N
S  H  J  R  U  U  R  I  T  E  K  Y  D  B  A
F  T  I  B  U  G  L  S  Z  I  M  V  L  E  L
J  U  C  H  V  F  Y  E  N  L  A  A  U  G  S
W  D  U  C  T  S  W  S  O  U  G  L  T  Z  O
T  O  N  S  I  L  S  Y  X  Q  K  L  M  E  N
B  T  S  K  M  Z  P  O  L  T  O  P  S  W  H
```

After you finish, check the answer key on page 112

Ex-SPLEEN What You Mean

Good work, Adventurers!

Now that you have learned all about the **lymphatic system**, let's put your knowledge to the test!

Fill in the blanks below.

Your lymphatic system helps your circulatory system and __ __ __ __ __ __ __

system do their jobs. The lymphatic system "cleans house" by maintaining your

__ __ __ __ __ __ __ __ __ __ __ __ __ and defending your body against __

__ __ __ __ __ __ and __ __ __ __ __ __ __ __. The five key components to the

lymphatic system are lymph, __ __ __ __ __ __ __ __ __ __ vessels, lymph

__ __ __ __ __, lymph organs, and __ __ __ __ __ __ __ __ __ __ __.

The lymphatic system journey to and from bloodstream first begins with lymph

vessels collecting __ __ __ __ __. Lymph travels through several lymph nodes

Inside the nodes, lymphocytes tag any __ __ __ __ __ __ __ __ __ __ for the immune

system to destroy.

The two last stops for lymph before entering the bloodstream are called the right

lymphatic __ __ __ __ __ and the __ __ __ __ __ __ __ __ duct.

After you finish, check the answer key on page 113.

Know Your Aztec Market

To Lymph and Let Buy

Markets were a very important part of Aztec life–so important, in fact, that the daily grand market at **Tlatelolco*** drew crowds as large as 60,000 people!

The well-developed Aztec economy and established trade routes were the foundation of these highly successful markets. Merchants and buyers traveled across the Aztec empire to buy, sell, and barter locally grown foods, handmade wares, and exotic garments from foreign lands. To barter is to exchange one item for another item of equal value, without using money.

> The most well-known form of Aztec currency was the cacao bean.

That's right! Cacao beans are best known today as the main ingredient in chocolate and cocoa, but to the Aztecs, the cacao bean was as valuable as money. They would bring cacao beans to the markets to buy items such as turkeys, chilies, pottery, firewood, jewelry, bird feathers, and medicines.

Cacao beans

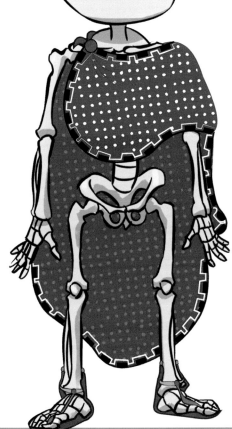

Merchants, known as **pochteca,*** were a vital part of Aztec society. Pochteca journeyed along the trade routes within and outside the empire to far-reaching cities, in order to find unique items that would make Montezuma himself smile! Pochteca were also given the task of gathering information from and sending messages to other villages. As a result, they were the empire's best source of communication.

One other important aspect of market culture was the opportunity for Aztecs to socialize. The markets were a great public space to meet with friends and neighbors to exchange news or to gossip about recent events.

Now imagine that you are at the grand market of Tlatelolco, in Tenochtitlan in your comic.

What do you see, hear, and smell? Do you taste the delicious flavors of ancient Central America?

_____

_____

_____

_____

*Say them like this:

tlatelolco - "tlah-tee-LOHL-ko"

pochteca - "poach-TEK-uh"

The strongest syllable is always shown in **CAPITALS** and **red**.

Know Your Appetite

Experience Mexican Cuisine

Agriculture was the largest part of the Aztec economy. All of Aztec society depended on the success of the crops that grew on the chinampas (*water garden*). The three main crops were corn, squash, and beans. Corn and beans are still two of the main ingredients used in Mexican cooking today.

Another popular food was chia, an edible seed that the Aztecs used to boost their energy. Today, chia is known as a healthy super food because of its high levels of protein and fiber.

The Aztec diet was mostly vegetarian, although they did fish, hunt wild game, and domesticate a few animals, such as turkeys and ducks. However, because the chinampas were so productive, the Aztecs were able to grow crops for millions of people. Nutrient- and protein-rich corn and beans became staples of the Aztec diet.

Corn   **Squash**   **Beans**

Pinky's Hint:

Read through the entire recipe. This way, you'll know what equipment and ingredients are needed, and you'll be familiar with the steps involved.

 Whenever you see the chef's hat icon, it means **you'll need an adult's help.**

Xitlacua cualli! *
(That means "Thanks for the food!" in Nahuatl.)

*Say it like this:

xitlacua cuali - "shee-tla-kwa-**KWA**-lee
The strongest syllable is always shown
in **CAPITALS** and **red**.

Recipes and food knowledge provided by
Chef Polly Legendre of La Gourmande Catering.

Mexican Hot Chocolate

Chocolate has been cherished in Mexico since it was discovered by the Aztec people.

They used the cacao bean (the main ingredient in chocolate) not only for food, but as a form of money as well.

The hot chocolate drink that the Aztecs enjoyed was very different from the kind that you have probably tried. Instead of sugar, the Aztecs mixed their chocolate with spices, peppers, and corn meal, making their hot chocolate less watery.

Today, many people still enjoy a traditional hot drink called "atole" that includes both chocolate and corn, and in some cases, cinnamon.

Prep Time:
5 minutes

Cooking Time:
5 minutes

Serves
4 People

Ingredients:

- 5–6 cups milk

- 1 round Mexican chocolate bar (Ibarra or Abuelita), broken into chunks

- 1 cinnamon stick

- 1 pinch nutmeg

Preparation:

1. Heat the milk in a saucepan over medium to low heat. While the milk is heating up, add the cinnamon stick and the pinch of nutmeg.

2. When the milk is hot, remove the cinnamon stick, add the chocolate, and whisk it vigorously until the chocolate is melted and the milk is frothy. Then it is ready to serve! You can use your cinnamon stick as a stir stick.

An alternate way of making this recipe is to pour the hot milk and the chocolate into a blender. Once in the blender, close the lid on tight and mix for 10 seconds or until all the chocolate is melted and mixed.

Aztec Vegetable Stew

As you've learned, the Aztec diet was mostly vegetarian and relied on staple vegetables and legumes like corn, squash, and beans. This recipe calls for all three – you'll really be eating like an Aztec once you finish this healthy and simple recipe.

**Prep Time:
10 minutes**

**Cooking time:
15-20 minutes**

**Serves
6-8 People**

Ingredients:

- 1 diced yellow or white onion

- 1 small zucchini, cut into roughly ¼-inch pieces

- 1 small yellow squash, cut into roughly ¼-inch pieces

- 1 cup green beans, trimmed and halved

- 1 medium green pepper, diced

- 2 cups fresh or frozen corn

- 1 can (14 oz) stewed tomatoes

- 1 tablespoon minced garlic

- 1 tablespoon olive oil or vegetable oil

- ½ teaspoon dried oregano

- Salt and pepper to taste

Preparation:

 1. Heat the olive oil in a large pan. Cook the garlic until fragrant.

 2. Add the onion, and cook until tender.

 3. Add the zucchini, yellow squash, green beans, and pepper. Cook for 5 minutes, stirring often.

 4. Add the corn, tomatoes, and oregano, and simmer for 10 minutes, stirring occasionally.

5. Season with salt and pepper to your taste.

6. You're ready to serve! You can eat this stew over rice, topped with shredded cheese (like queso fresco or Monterey Jack), in warm corn tortillas, or on its own. Enjoy!

 Show off your cooking skills!
Have your grown-up take a photo, and share on social media using the hashtag:

#KnowYourAdventure

 **KnowYourselfOAK**   **KnowYourselfOAK**

Thoughts for Young Chefs

What did you learn about Mexican food that you didn't know before this adventure?

_____

_____

_____

Know Yourself Adventure Recipes

Review the recipes from previous adventures and choose a destination to compare. Record similarities and differences in the Venn Diagram at right.

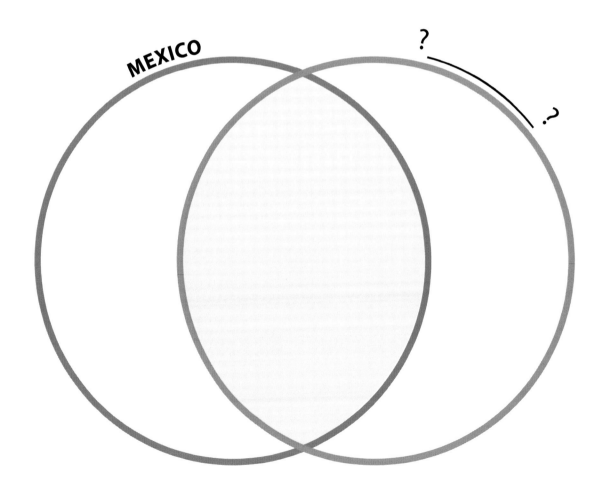

MEXICO

?

?

What type of food are you inspired to make next?

_____

_____

_____

_____

_____

_____

_____

Show off your cooking skills!

Have your grown-up take a photo, and
share on social media using the hashtag:

#KnowYourAdventure

KnowYourselfOAK   KnowYourselfOAK

Connect the Lymph Nodes

Adventurer, great job working your way through this guide.

In this adventure you learned all about your lymphatic system.
**Do you remember what the lymphatic system does?
Write your answer below!**

_____

_____

_____

_____

_____

Based on what you know about ancient Aztecs, what activities did they participate in that helped move lymph throughout their bodies?

_____

_____

_____

To keep your lymphatic system healthy you need to move your lymph!
What are some ways you can do to move your lymph?
(See page 82 for one example)

_____

_____

_____

_____

_____

_____

_____

_____

_____

Did you know that a massage is a great way to move your lymph?
Try giving your parent one to start off their day and see how they feel!

THE SEVENTH SENSE

Are you sure you want to do this?

Naz, I've never been more sure of anything in my life.

Buster!

Okay, boy, now maybe we'll be able to understand each other.

Did it work?

Buster, can you understand me, boy?

...

Well, we tried.

I'll have two pepperoni pizzas, a side of buffalo wings, and two orders of cheese sticks. Extra cheese.

Further Reading

Fiction

Readers can enjoy exploring Ancient Aztec history as they travel through this 'Choose Your Own Adventure'. Dive into Ancient Aztec culture in this suspenseful read - perfect for younger readers.

Raum, Elizabeth. The Aztec Empire: *An Interactive History Adventure*. Capstone Press, 2012. (Ages 7-11)

A mystery to keep your reader's guessing, this story follows Paloma Marquez as she searches for a missing ring in Mexico City. For those interested in the more recent history of Mexico this provides an exciting and engaging tale.

Cervantes, Angela. *Me, Frida, and the Secret of the Peacock Ring*. Scholastic, 2018

Non-Fiction

An introduction to the life and times of the Aztec people as they came into contact with Europe, this book presents non-fiction through the guise of a newspaper, providing short bites of information with a fun layout and colorful illustrations.

Steele, Philip. History News: *The Aztec News. Candlewick*, 2009 (Ages 9-12)

Rady Children's Hospital, San Diego is a great online resource to continue learning about the Lymphatic system. This site and other children's hospital sites make learning about the body's system and illnesses a fun and educational experience for kids.

https://www.rchsd.org/health-articles/spleen-and-lymphatic-system/

So who are we waiting for again?

The soil tester.

To make sure our site is ready for construction.

The dirt looks good to me.

Looks can be deceiving. Especially if where you're looking is on the surface.

PUFF

Well goooooood morning!

coloring opportunity

11 NEXT
The Nervous System

KN⊕W YOURSELF

11

The Nervous System
Keep Calm and Neuron

GUADALCANAL

You and the Time Skaters travel back to the Second World War in order to help their new friends, the Navajo Code talkers! Learn about the nervous system, and experience one of the most compelling stories in history

You and the Time Skaters travel back to the Second World War to help their new friends, the Navajo Code talkers! Learn about the nervous system, and experience one of the most compelling stories in history. . .

Answer Keys

Aztec-nically Speaking

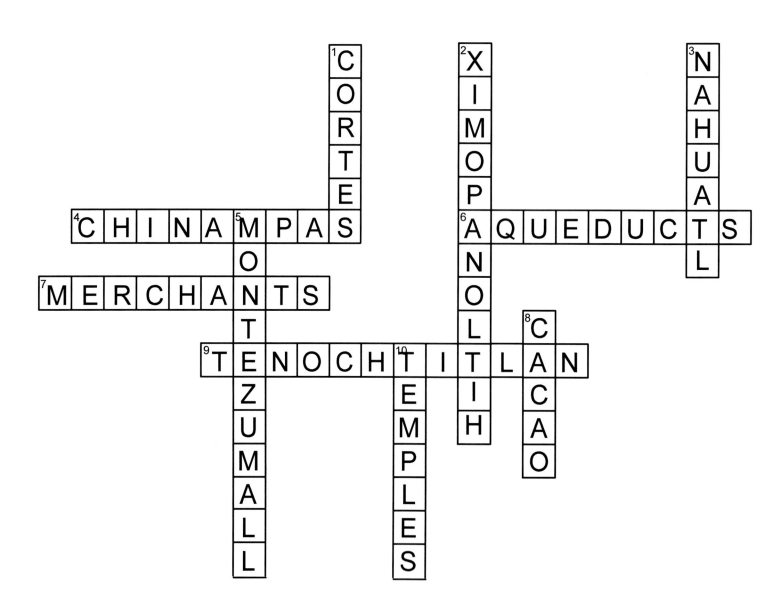

Ancient Aztec Answers

The Aztecs started building their capital T E N O C H T I T L A N

in 1325. While the location started as a small island, they expanded it with

C H I N A M P A S, a type of floating garden. At its height the city was

F I V E square miles and had a population of over F I V E million. One of

the most impressive engineering accomplishments carried fresh water for people

to drink and to water crops called an A Q U E D U C T.

The ninth ruler of Tenochtitlan was named M O N T E Z U M A I I. The

Aztec Empire under him stretched from the P A C I F I C ocean to the

Gulf of M E X I C O. The palace contained hanging G A R D E N S,

pools and even a private Z O O. Many of these accomplishments were possible

because of the advanced M A T H used by the Atzec people.

The Aztecs used a massive calendar called the S U N S T O N E which

was carved into solid R O C K. This combined two systems, the Xiuhpohualli

which tracked the S U N and the Tonalpohualli which counted D A Y S.

These two combined to create the Aztec calendar, which wouldn't repeat a date

for F I F T Y - T W O years.

Locate Lost Lymphocytes Word Search

```
I G Y S P L E E N F L C Q H T
B N D N A U K L Y M P H U T Y
V A T V I R U S U S H Q R H G
E X L E T C Z S E H G W B Y E
S C P A R B A C T E R I A M R
S X A E N S P M M T C N S U M
E P M P Y C T E Z G N P B S I
L Z W F S E E I D J K O T Z N
S H J R U U R I T E K Y D B A
F T I B U G L S Z I M V L E L
J U C H V F Y E N L A A U G S
W D U C T S W S O U G L T Z O
T O N S I L S Y X Q K L M E N
B T S K M Z P O L T O P S W H
```

Ex-SPLEEN What You Mean

Your lymphatic system helps your circulatory system and I M M U N E

system do their jobs. The lymphatic system "cleans house" by maintaining your

B L O O D   P R E S S U R E and defending your body against

V I R U S E S and B A C T E R I A. The five key components to the

lymphatic system are lymph, L Y M P H A T I C vessels, lymph

N O D E S, lymph organs, and L Y M P H O C Y T E S.

The lymphatic system journey to and from bloodstream first begins with lymph

vessels collecting L Y M P H. Lymph travels through several lymph nodes

Inside the nodes, lymphocytes tag any I N V A D E R S for the immune

system to destroy.

The two last stops for lymph before entering the bloodstream are called the right

lymphatic D U C T S and the T H O R A C I C duct.

Bonus Challenge

NAHUATL: Xiuhpohualli and Tonalpohualli

SPANISH: veintenas and trecenas

Your Lymphatic System

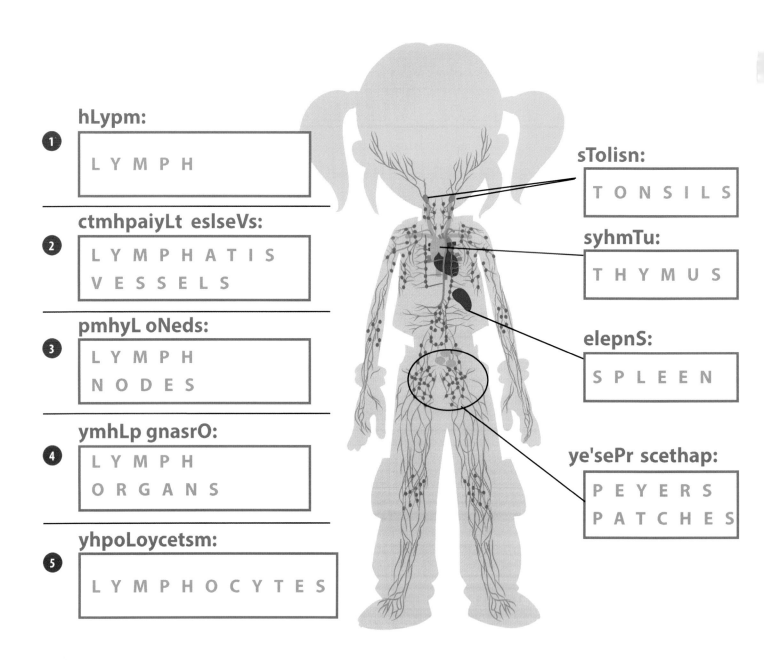

hLypm:

1 L Y M P H

ctmhpaiyLt eslseVs:

2 L Y M P H A T I S
V E S S E L S

pmhyL oNeds:

3 L Y M P H
N O D E S

ymhLp gnasrO:

4 L Y M P H
O R G A N S

yhpoLoycetsm:

5 L Y M P H O C Y T E S

sTolisn:

T O N S I L S

syhmTu:

T H Y M U S

elepnS:

S P L E E N

ye'sePr scethap:

P E Y E R S
P A T C H E S

CREATED WITH LOVE
BY THE
KNOW YOURSELF TEAM